THE
COOK
BOOK

ANNE SWABEY

The author's royalties for this book are all being
donated to the Leanora Children's Cancer Fund.

Illustrated by Linda Thomas

*I would like to dedicate this book to all the mothers
and fathers, medical staff and back-up groups who
dedicate their lives to helping children with terrible
diseases. Having recently been to hospital with my
own children, and had the privilege of seeing them
walking out happy, strong and healthy, I feel that one
should not forget those left behind. So, in buying this
book, I hope you have done two things: become
enthusiastic cooks, and donated some money to those
less fortunate children who, through no fault of their
own, cannot enjoy the many things we take for
granted.*

*A big thank you to my own husband and children -
Charles, Annabel and Lavinia - who have been
guinea pigs for many a recipe, and another thank you
to Tizzie Dennet who proved an invaluable back-up!*

Note on the Author:
Anne has a diploma in advanced cooking from the
Elizabeth Russel Cookery School. She worked for
the directors' dinning room of NatWest for four
years, and has worked as a freelance caterer for
many London companies. She now runs cookery
classes for children and young adults. This is Anne's
first book.

The author's royalties for this book are being donated
to:
        The Leanora Children's Cancer Fund
        Broadlands
        Romsey
        Hampshire
        FO51 9ZD

CONTENTS

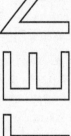

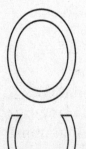

INTRODUCTION

I didn't learn to cook until I was eighteen. After leaving school, I attended a number of cookery schools but, as in most walks of life, I learnt the real art of cooking from practical experience. I believe the famous chef Prue Leith learnt to cook by starting on page one of a very large recipe book and working her way through the whole volume.

Do not worry about making mistakes. Remember that even great chefs make mistakes. They usually occur when you are hurrying and don't concentrate.

It is tempting to rush into the recipe without reading it properly. Of course it is fun to experiment with different ingredients. When you are starting to cook, however, it really does pay to read the recipe and follow it exactly. As you become more practised, you will have the basic skills at your fingertips and can build on them.

It is rather like learning a language – you have to grasp a lot of grammar and vocabulary in the early days.

With cooking, you learn the basic recipes first - which is much more fun!

Never be afraid to ask for help. I'm sure mum or dad would be delighted, and as you become more experienced you can pay them back by telling them to put their feet up, because you will make supper.

Other nationalities have been very rude about English cookery in the past, so let's change all that. Get in the kitchen and create! Put away those convenience foods. Fresh food (vegetables or wonderful salads) is far more nutritious and delicious. If you don't feel like cooking anything elaborate, stick to something very simple. Using fresh ingredients, you'll be amazed at how many compliments you receive.

Above all, enjoy yourself. Invite a friend round to join you: cooking with someone else is always fun. The wonderful thing about cooking is that after all that work, there is all that eating!

If you are happy with what you have cooked, that is the most important thing. Everyone has different tastes. Some people prefer savoury and some sweet. Have confidence in yourself and 'Bon Appetit'.

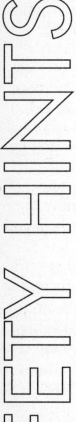

Don't start cooking, especially any recipe involving heat or sharp knives, unless there is an adult near that you could call to for help.

◆ The first thing to do when you start is to wash your hands and make sure the chopping board and work surface are spotlessly clean. You can use one of the new anti-bacterial sprays as a safety measure. Be especially careful when cooking chicken - always wash your hands before and after.

◆ Never run in the kitchen. It is easy to fall or slip and knock into something hot.

◆ Remember that knives are extremely dangerous. Never leave one in a washing-up bowl. It is possible for someone else to come along and put their hands in the soapy water without realising there is a knife there.

◆ Always hold a knife blade downwards and cut into a chopping board. Never walk around with a knife in your hand.

◆ Always use oven gloves to move items in or out of the oven. Use great caution when opening the oven door and remember to turn everything off when you have finished.

◆ Be very careful carrying hot food, as you could spill it over yourself.

◆ When using an electric plug make sure the socket is turned off and your hands are completely dry.

◆ Never leave saucepan handles turned out towards you. Push them to one side so no one can knock them as they pass.

◆ If you burn yourself, put the burn under cold running water for at least 10 minutes. Don't put lotion on the burn. Call for help and get the burn checked.

◆ If you have a cut, wash the cut and cover it with a plaster. Even very superficial cuts on the hands can bleed a great deal, so be very careful. If the cut bleeds a lot, clean the cut, press the edges of the cut together, preferably with a clean dressing, and go for help.

◆ Always wear an apron to protect your clothes.

Having been let loose in the kitchen this time, you are more likely to be allowed in again if you wash all the dirty dishes and clean the work surfaces.

Listed below are the basic items you will need, but as you gain in experience, it is fun to build up a whole 'batterie de cuisine'. Every cook has their own favourite gadgets. I can spend hours browsing in a cookery shop, looking at all the wonderful things, and they are fun items to ask for as Christmas or birthday presents. If you look after them, most things should last a lifetime. My own favourite piece of equipment is my food processor and if you are lucky enough to have access to one, you will find many recipe times cut in half. If you are able to use one, be careful with the blade and leave it for an adult to wash up.

2 wooden spoons
Sieve
Small, medium and large mixing bowls
Frying pan spatula (also called a fish slice)
Rubber spatula
Teaspoon, knife, fork and spoon
Chopping board

Small knife

Large knife (both should be very sharp)

Measuring jug

Scales

Cooking Rack

Balloon whisk

Cheese grater

Palate knife

Oven gloves

Apron

Frying pan

Milk pan

Casserole dish

Large/small saucepan

Colander

Potato peeler

Kitchen scissors

Can opener

2 Cake tins

Juice extractor

Tongs

2 Baking trays

Potato masher

Pastry brush

Rolling pin

Tin foil

Grease-proof paper

Clingfilm

CONVERSION CHART

Imperial		Metric	Imperial		Metric
1 lb	=	450 gms	9 oz	=	250 gms
1 oz	=	25 gms	10 oz	=	275 gms
2 oz	=	50 gms	11 oz	=	300 gms
3 oz	=	75 gms	12 oz	=	325/350 gms
4 oz	=	100/125 gms	13 oz	=	375gms
5 oz	=	150 gms	14 oz	=	400 gms
6 oz	=	175 gms	15 oz	=	425 gms
7 oz	=	200 gms	16 oz/1 lb =		450 gms
8 oz	=	225 gms	11/2 lbs =		700 gms

These are some quick measurements to save you going to the scales each time you wish to measure something . It is important to try and be as accurate as possible.

1 oz flour = 25 gms = 3 level tbls

1 oz sugar = 25 gms = 2 level tbls

1 oz icing sugar = 25 gms = 3 level tbls

1 oz butter = 25 gms = 2 level tbls

1 oz grated cheese = 25 gms = 4 level tbls

3 teaspoons = 1 tablespoon

To measure golden syrup warm a spoon, dip a piece of kitchen towel into oil so it absorbs a little and rub it over the spoon. Then measure the syrup in the spoon and it will pour off without sticking.
To measure a level spoonful, scoop the ingredients on to the spoon and smooth the surface with the back of a knife.
Liquids can be measured with a measuring jug. Read the

measurements at eye level so you can be sure to get an accurate reading.

When using scales, always make sure you can read the scales at eye level, so you can be sure of getting an accurate reading.

Take the bag of flour or sugar to the scales to be weighed - this avoids spillages and more mess to clear up later on.

TEMPERATURES

°F	°C	Gas Mark	
250	130	1/2	Very Cool
275	140	1	Very Cool
300	150	2	Cool
325	160/170	3	Warm
350	180	4	Moderate
375	190	5	Fairly Hot
400	200	6	Fairly Hot
425	210/220	7	Hot
450	230	8	Very Hot
475	240	9	Very Hot

I have found this chart very helpful.

PLANNING A MENU

When deciding what to cook for your family or friends, there are four main things to remember:

1. Colour of the food
2. Texture of the food
3. Taste of the food
4. Fruit and vegetables in season

COLOUR When thinking of a menu, think of the colour of the food. It is boring to have a plate of food which is all the same colour, or three courses which all look the same. For example, cabbage, green beans and peas would look dull together, as would chicken, rice and cauliflower. It would be more interesting to choose, say, carrots with green beans and potatoes. You can add a little colour to make a dull dish more exciting. A plain food, like tuna fish paté, can be made to look nicer with a sprig of watercress or a lettuce twist.

TEXTURE Try to vary the foods you are serving so that some are crunchy and some soft. An omelette with mashed potatoes would be heavy-going. It would be much more appetising to serve it with a crisp green salad. Ask yourself as you work out the menu: is it soft, hard or crunchy, and have I got a good mixture of all three textures?

TASTE Try to 'taste' your menu in your head when you are planning it. It would be uninspiring to serve melon as a first course and a fresh fruit salad for dessert. In the same way, it would be too much to serve a rich, heavy pudding after a heavy main course, even if the food itself was cooked to perfection.

FOOD IN SEASON Try to find out what foods are in season. This should be clear from the selection available at your local market or greengrocer, and the cost of the food is a good guide. It is possible to buy most items at any time of the year but you will get the best flavours from the food in season. Strawberries and raspberries do taste better on a hot summer day, just as plums and nectarines taste better in the autumn. Imported vegetables have often had to travel many miles, and so cannot be as fresh as our home-grown produce.

All in all try to maintain a balance. Ask yourself these three questions:

Have I got the colour right?

Is all the food soft or all hard?

How will it taste?

The first thing to do when reading a recipe is to make sure you have all the ingredients and then ask someone if you may use them.

It is important to work out what time you want to eat, so that you can be sure you have plenty of time to prepare and cook the food.

Having decided on your recipe, check to see what temperature your oven should be at and turn it on. Certain recipes, especially cakes and biscuits, are unlikely to succeed if you put them into a cold oven.

Wash your hands before handling any food.

Assemble all the ingredients, measure and weigh all of them and double-check that nothing is missing. Recipes sometimes fail because one of the vital ingredients has been omitted. Also check that you have all the necessary equipment.

When the recipe refers to weight, most cook books give measurements in both metric grammes and imperial ounces. It is important to choose which measurement you will use and not to mix them up. Check your scales to see whether they measure in metric or imperial. Most do both nowadays but the old fashioned ones (like mine) measure only in imperial.

Before starting, read the recipe through to check you are able to cope with all the individual stages. Then work through the whole recipe carefully and slowly, following the instructions, and you will be very pleased with the results.

DECORATION

You could try:
Watercress sprigs
Parsley sprigs or Mint
Lemon twists
Black olives
Tomatoes
Peppers, chopped and blanched
Radishes
Spring onions

Try and keep decorations very simple. One can go to the extreme of having a plate covered in decorations, so the end effect looks a mess. When in doubt leave it out!

M

ost of us know how to lay a table for an informal family supper or lunch, but it is useful to know the correct way on more formal occasions, so that you can impress your friends or give mum or dad a surprise dinner party! The correct way is logical: you start with the first course cutlery on the very outside and then work your way in as the courses progress. If you were going to start with soup, you would put the soup spoon on the outside, right hand side. If you are having rolls and butter you should put a small knife next to the soup spoon. Then you place the large knife for the main course on the right and a large fork on the left hand side. Finally add the dessert spoon and fork, with the dessert spoon on the right hand side and fork on the left. If you are short of space on the table, you can put the spoon and fork at the top of the place setting, with the fork handle to the left hand and the spoon handle to the right hand. (I used to remember this by saying 'fork and fork never meet'.)

The small bread plate goes on the left hand side and the napkin goes on top of the plate. Glasses are placed on the right above the knives.

dessert spoon

glass

dessert fork

bread plate

soup spoon

large plate

napkin

large fork

small knife

large knife

TECHNIQUES

Here are a few basic techniques that I hope will help you when reading the recipes in this book.

BEATING

This means mixing food as fast as you can with a wooden spoon or an electric whisk in order to introduce air into your mixture. The harder you beat the more successful the outcome will be.

WHISKING

Whisking is a faster way of beating and is done with a balloon whisk, a rotary whisk or an electric whisk. Again the idea is to introduce as much air into the ingredients as is possible.

FRYING ONIONS

A great many recipes use fried onions so I feel it is worth a special note.

Cut the top and bottom off the onion and peel off all the brown skins. Cut the onion in half and slice each half. Put the butter (or cooking oil) into a pan and melt over a low heat. Add the chopped onion and coat with the melted butter, i.e. mix in pan with butter. Keep them over a very low heat so you can just hear that they are cooking. Keep turning them over so they cook on all sides.

It does take quite a long time to cook onions, but it is worth taking time over them because if you burn them they will be too bitter and spoil the entire recipe.

Onions become almost transparent when they are cooked and that is the time to add the other ingredients, or to remove them from the heat.

SEPARATING AN EGG

Many people are frightened of doing this but there is an easy trick! Crack the egg on to a saucer, place one half of the egg shell over the yolk and pour off the white into the bowl you wish to use. Or crack the egg and pour the contents through your fingers catching the egg yolk as you do it.

When you are separating eggs in order to whisk the egg whites, it is most important that the bowl and whisk are very clean and that there is no egg yolk mixed with your egg white.

ROLLING OUT PASTRY

Make the pastry and knead gently into a ball. Sprinkle flour on the work surface and rolling pin. Push the pastry down with the rolling pin making three dents, turn the pastry round and make three more dents, so you have a round shape. Roll away from you and turn the pastry round, then roll away from you again. If you keep repeating this, you should end up with an approximate circle.

Measure your flan dish on top of the pastry. You need about 2 inches overlap. Wrap the pastry over the rolling pin and roll it over your flan case. Push the pastry well into all the edges. If it is splitting, patch it up with pastry from an area that has too much.

Trim off the overlap with a sharp knife. Leave the pastry in the fridge for half an hour to rest.

BAKING BLIND

This is a term for pre-cooking pastry. If you are going to pre-cook the pastry, prick the base all over with a fork in order to stop the pastry rising when it is cooking, thus making it very difficult to fill your flan dish.

If you have baking beans, put some grease-proof paper on top of the pastry and sprinkle beans over the grease-proof paper. Place in the oven. Alternatively use tin foil. Cook at 180 C for 10 minutes then remove the tin foil or beans and cook for a further 10 minutes, or until the pastry is golden brown.

BROWNING

Before you put red meat or chicken into a casserole to cook it is important to fry it quickly in a little oil or butter. This seals the meat so that the juices will not run out (which makes the meat tough). It also gives the meat a golden-brown colouring which looks much more appetising.

Put the oil or butter on the heat - the recipe will give you the quantity. Wait until you can hear it sizzling, add the meat to the pan and fry for about 2 minutes on each side, or until the meat has changed colour.

Mince has a high fat content, so when I brown mince I warm the frying pan first and then add the mince, but I don't add any extra oil. You need to keep stirring to stop the meat sticking to the pan.

KNEADING

This is a necessary process in bread making. Once you have made your bread dough, it is important to knead it to help the bread rise. Put your dough on to a lightly floured work surface and pull it and push it as much as you can for about 10 minutes. (Think of that teacher who gave you too much homework and this will help you!)

SEASONING

This is a term for the addition of salt and pepper. The amount used in recipes is only intended as a guide. We all tend to use too much salt, so if you can try to reduce the amount used. This is no bad thing!
Always use a little salt and pepper first and test. It is easy to put more in but impossible to take it out. If, however, you do put in too much, put a

peeled potato into your sauce or soup whilst cooking, and this will absorb some of the salt.

SHORTCRUST PASTRY

8 oz/225 gms flour
2 oz/50 gms cookeen/lard
2 oz/50 gms margarine/butter
pinch of salt
3 tbls cold water

Sieve the flour and salt together into a bowl.
Chop the lard and margarine into small pieces.
With very clean hands, rub the margarine and lard into the flour with your fingers (not your palms). Another method is to take two knives and cut the mixture in opposite directions.
Either way, keep mixing until the mixture looks like breadcrumbs. Add cold water and mix with a palate knife.
Gather the dough together with your hands.
Turn it on to a floured chopping board and knead it gently. Shape the pastry into a round ball, cover with cling film or grease-proof paper and leave it in the fridge for at least half an hour.

Practically anything can go into a salad. It is a wonderful way of using up leftover vegetables or meat. By giving them a really good coating of french dressing or mayonnaise, or indeed a mixture of both, and putting them on a bed of lettuce, you have a quick and delicious meal.

Here are some ingredient ideas for a few salads:

GREEN SALAD
Lettuce
Watercress
Cucumber
Spring onions
Chives
Avocado

MIXED SALAD
Tomatoes
Cucumber
Radishes
Lettuce
Cooked beetroot
Peppers
Sliced hard boiled egg

CHEF'S SALAD
Lettuce
- shredded
Chicken
- diced and cooked
Ham
- diced and cooked
Grated Cheese
Cucumber
Streaky Bacon
- cook until it is really crispy
and crumble it over the top

RICE SALAD
Cooked rice
Cucumber
- chopped
Cooked peas
Red peppers
- de-seeded and chopped
Peanuts
Parsley

These are just some examples. I haven't put any quantities down as there are no set rules governing a salad. You can have fun inventing your own mixture and naming it after your favourite place or person.

VEGETABLES

I was once told a useful tip for cooking vegetables, which I will now pass on to you: vegetables that grow under the ground go into cold salted water with the lid on, and are then brought to the boil. Vegetables that grow above the ground are cooked in boiling salted water with the lid off. (As always, there are exceptions to the rule - new potatoes are put into boiling water.) If you are unsure, it is a useful tip to remember.
The smaller the vegetables, the quicker they cook.

Here are a few cooking times:

Cauliflower & Broccoli
> boiling water
> 10 minutes

Brussel Sprouts
> boiling water
> 10 minutes

French Beans
> boiling water
> 6 minutes

Carrots	whole	cold water 10 minutes
	sliced into small pieces	cold water 5 minutes
Peas	frozen	5 minutes
Potatoes	new	boiling water 20 minutes
	old	cold water 20 minutes
Cabbage	sliced	boiling water 8 minutes

As with all foods different people like different things. I prefer most vegetables to be slightly hard. You may like them very well done. The above times are only a guide and with practice you will establish your own cooking times.

PASTA & RICE

There are many varieties of pasta and rice available in shops and it is always best to follow the instructions on the packets, especially with the quick-cook varieties.

These are the basic ways to cook them:

PASTA
Allow 3 oz/75 gms of pasta per person.
For 4 people:

12 oz/325/350 gms of pasta.

2 tsp salt

1 tsp oil

4 pints water

Add the salt and oil to the water, bring it to the boil and add the pasta. If you are cooking spaghetti, hold the end of a bunch and push it gently into the water. It will slide down as the water softens it. Keep the water at a steady boil for 12 minutes, stirring occasionally with a fork (be careful not to scratch the pan). Drain the pasta into a colander. The cooking oil in the water stops the pasta sticking together.

RICE

I would suggest that, until you are experienced, you buy the *'easy cook'* rice. Once you get used to that, you can experiment with other varieties.

For 4 people:

8 oz/225 gms rice

2 tsp salt

4 pints water

Bring the salted water to the boil. Add the rice and allow the water to boil gently, stirring it occasionally with a fork for about 15 minutes. Drain the rice into a colander.

Brown rice will take twice as long as white rice to cook. It is firmer than white rice when cooked.

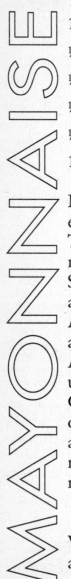

MAYONNAISE

1 egg yolk

¼ level tsp salt

½ level tsp mustard

¼ level tsp pepper

¼ pint vegetable oil

1 tbls vinegar or lemon juice

Make sure all the ingredients and equipment are at room temperature. The mayonnaise will curdle if this is not done.

Separate the egg yolk from the white and put the egg yolk in a bowl.

Add salt, pepper, mustard and vinegar and gently whisk with balloon whisk.

Add 1 tsp of measured oil and whisk until blended.

Continue this step-by-step until all the oil has been absorbed. Once you have achieved the consistency of mayonnaise, the oil can be added at the rate of one tablespoon.

WARNING: Only add the oil a little at a time. If you become impatient and add the oil too quickly, it will curdle. If it does curdle, put another egg yolk into a clean bowl and add the curdled mixture to this, little by little, whisking as you do. If you feel the mayonnaise is too thick, a dessertspoon of boiling water can be added to make it thinner.

FRENCH DRESSING

1 tsp french mustard

¼ tsp salt

black pepper

¼ level tsp sugar (optional)

1 tbls vinegar

1 tbls salad oil

½ tsp crushed garlic (optional)

1 tsp chopped fresh mixed herbs (optional)

Put the salt, pepper, mustard, sugar, garlic, herbs and vinegar into a bowl and stir. Whisk the oil into the ingredients gradually.
French dressing will separate if it is left to stand, so before you pour it over your salad give it a good stir or whisk.

WHITE SAUCE

1oz/25gms butter
1oz/25gms flour
½ pint milk
(Use ¾oz/15gms of butter and flour for thin sauce, 2oz/50gms of both for thick, as you prefer.)

Put the butter into a saucepan and melt it over a low heat. When the butter is foaming, add the flour. Beat the two together really well. Add the milk very slowly, beating thoroughly each time you add a spoonful. The mixture should boil each time you add milk.

CHEESE SAUCE
2 oz/50 gms mature cheddar cheese
1 tsp ready-made mustard
Add these to ½ pint of white sauce, after you have taken it off the heat.

PARSLEY SAUCE
Instead of the cheese, add 2 tablespoons of parsley to ½ pint of white sauce.

TIP: If you want to leave the sauce to stand, float some milk on the top. This will stop a skin forming. When you are ready to use it, simply mix the milk in.

THE SYMBOLS

OVEN TEMPERATURE

COOKED ON THE HOB

RECIPE FEEDS...

EASY
1

MEDIUM
2

DIFFICULT
3

ABBREVIATIONS:
tbl - tablespoon
tsp - teaspoon
oz - ounce
gm - gramme
l - litre
ml - millilitre
lb - pound

PIZZA

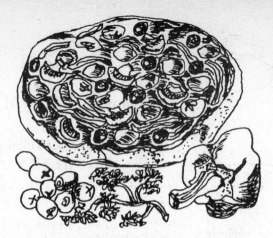

INGREDIENTS

BASE 4 oz/100 gms plain flour
½ level tsp salt
½ level tsp dried instant yeast
2 fluid oz/50 gms warm water
(You can use a packet mix if you've never made dough before.)

1 Sift flour into a bowl. Add the salt and yeast. Make a hole in the middle and pour in the warm water.

2 Stir all the ingredients together gently. You will eventually need to use your hands.

3 Turn the mixture on to a floured board and knead it as hard as you can.

TOPPINGS

1 tbls cooking oil
¼ onion
1 small tin chopped tomatoes
½ level tsp castor sugar
1 tsp mixed herbs

Choice of: Olives, Mozzarella Cheese, Mushrooms, sliced, Chopped Ham, Peppers thinly sliced, grated Cheddar Cheese.

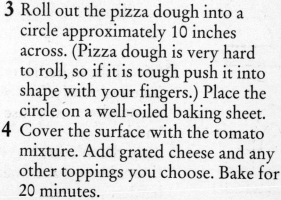

1 Chop the onion into very small pieces, and put it into a saucepan with herbs, tomatoes, sugar, and salt and pepper (¼ tsp of each).

2 Put a lid on the saucepan and simmer the sauce for 20 minutes. Stir it occasionally to prevent it sticking to the pan. Then remove it from the heat.

3 Roll out the pizza dough into a circle approximately 10 inches across. (Pizza dough is very hard to roll, so if it is tough push it into shape with your fingers.) Place the circle on a well-oiled baking sheet.

4 Cover the surface with the tomato mixture. Add grated cheese and any other toppings you choose. Bake for 20 minutes.

SODA BREAD

INGREDIENTS

1 lb/450 gms plain flour
2 level tsp bicarbonate of soda
2 level tsp cream of tartar
1 level tsp salt
1 oz/25 gms lard
½ pint buttermilk (or ½ pint milk and 1 tbl lemon juice)

1 Sieve flour, bicarbonate of soda, cream of tartar and salt into a bowl. Cut the lard into small pieces and rub it in with your fingers until it has the consistency of breadcrumbs.

220°C
425 F
Gas M7

2 Make a hole in the flour mixture. Pour in the buttermilk and mix with a wooden spoon.

3 Once it is rubbed in, use your hands to mix the dough into a ball. Turn it out on to a floured surface and shape it into a circle approximately 7 inches/18 cm across. Grease a baking sheet and put the dough on to it.

1

4 Make a cross on the top of the dough with the point of a knife. Bake it in the oven for 30 minutes until well risen and golden.

5 Remove from the oven and leave to cool on a wire rack.

Eat it while it is still warm, spread with butter. You may find it rather plain on its own, but it is delicious with soup.

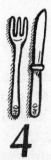

4

HAMBURGERS

INGREDIENTS

1 lb/450 gms extra lean mince
beef
1 egg
1 tsp mixed dried herbs
1 tsp garlic puree/ 1 clove
garlic (optional)
1 tsp frozen chopped parsley
4 hamburger buns

1 Put the mince in a bowl.
Crack the egg into the bowl
and mix it into the mince with
a wooden spoon.

2 Add ½ tsp salt, the herbs, garlic, parsley and some pepper and stir the mixture thoroughly.

3 With very clean hands, divide the mixture into four. Shape each one into a flat round shape.

4 Chill them in the fridge (preferably overnight) so they keep their shape while you are cooking them.

5 Turn the grill on full and grill each side for about 5 minutes. Turn them over with tongs or a spatula.

1

6 Turn the grill off, remove the burgers and put them into buns.

You can add your favourite fillings (cheese, lettuce, tomato ketchup, etc).

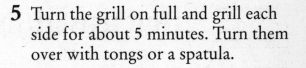

4

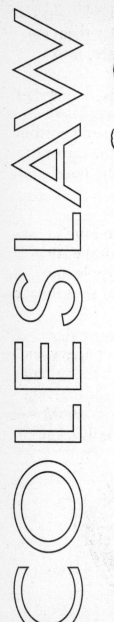

COLESLAW

INGREDIENTS

¼ white cabbage
3 carrots
1 eating apple
1 stick celery
1 tbls sultanas (optional)
1 tbls peanuts (optional)
2 tbls french dressing
2 tbls mayonnaise

1 With one hand press the cut side of the cabbage down on to a chopping board. Carefully slice the leaves into shreds.

2 Wash the cabbage and celery in a bowl of cold water. Dry them in a clean tea towel. Put them into a large mixing bowl.

3 Peel the carrots with a potato peeler. Slice off the top and bottom of each carrot. Grate the carrot (be very careful not to grate your fingertips!).

4 Peel the apple, cut into four sections, and scoop out the core with a knife. Cut the apple into small pieces and add to the cabbage and carrot mixture.

5 Finally slice the stick of celery and add it to the bowl with the sultanas and peanuts. Pour on the dressing and mayonnaise and mix all the ingredients together well.

TOAD IN THE HOLE

INGREDIENTS

4 oz/100 gms plain flour
½ tsp salt
¼ pint milk and ¼ pint
water mixed together
2 eggs
8 sausages
2 tbls vegetable oil

1 Sift the flour and salt into a large mixing bowl. Make a hole in the middle.

2 Break two eggs into a cup and beat them with a fork. Pour them into a measuring jug with the milk and water.

3 Pour 1/2 the egg mixture into the hole in the flour. Then with a whisk, gently stir the egg/milk mixture into the flour. When it has all been mixed in, gently whisk in the remaining liquid. There should be no lumps in it. This mixture is now called batter.

4 Cut the sausages in half and place them in your baking dish. Pour over 2 tbls of oil and place them in the hot oven for 5 minutes.

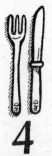

5 Very carefully lift the baking dish out of the oven with your oven gloves. The oil should be **very hot** to cook the batter properly. Pour the batter over the sausages. Bake the dish for 35-40 minutes, until the batter is well risen and golden brown.

CHOCOLATE CHIP COOKIE

INGREDIENTS

4 oz/100 gms butter
6 oz/175 gms self raising flour
2 oz/50 gms soft light brown sugar
2 oz/50 gms soft dark brown sugar
1 tsp vanilla essence
1 egg
8 oz/225 gms cooking chocolate/chocolate chips

1 Preheat the oven.

2 If you are using a block of chocolate, put it in a plastic bag and break it into very small pieces with a rolling pin.

180°C
350°F
Gas M4

3 Grease two baking sheets very well.

4 Mix the sugar with the butter and beat thoroughly. Stir in the vanilla essence.

5 Break the egg into a little bowl and mix with a fork. Add this egg a little at a time into the mixture, remembering to beat it with your wooden spoon.

1

6 Sift the flour into the mixture. Add chocolate chips.

7 Use two teaspoons to spoon the mixture on to the baking tray, leaving plenty of space between them. (Since the mixture makes approximately 30 cookies, it is easier to bake them in two batches.)

8 Bake the cookies in the oven for about 8 minutes. They should be a light golden brown when finished.

9 Use a spatula to remove them from the baking tray and on to a cooling rack. Store in an air-tight container.

INGREDIENTS

6 cubes strawberry jelly
¼ pint double cream
5 oz/150 gms strawberry
yoghurt (1 small pot)
1 small can strawberries
1 dessert spoon castor sugar
200 ml water

1 Strain the liquid off the
strawberries.

2 Put the jelly cubes and water
into a small saucepan and stir
over a gentle heat until the
cubes have melted. When the

46

1

jelly cubes have completely
dissolved, remove the pan from the
heat and set to one side to cool.

3 Put the yoghurt, double cream and
sugar into a bowl and whisk
together well.

4 When the jelly mixture is quite
cool, whisk it into the
cream /yoghurt mixture.
Fold in the strawberries.

5 Put the mixture in the fridge for
2 hours to set.

4

*Serve with whipped cream. You can
use fresh strawberries in this, but
they will not keep as well.*

HOT FRUIT KEBABS

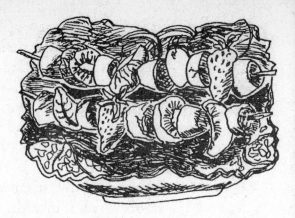

INGREDIENTS

6 tbls creme fraiche
4 tbls soft dark brown sugar
a little melted butter
marshmallows
Suggested fruit: grapes,
strawberries, bananas, kiwi
fruit, mandarin oranges

1 Mix the creme fraiche with
2 tbls brown sugar in a bowl.
Allow the sugar to melt and
then give the mixture a very
thorough stir.

2 Wash the grapes and
strawberries. Peel the

1

bananas, mandarin oranges and kiwi fruit. Cut the kiwis and bananas into large chunks.

3 Thread the fruit and marshmallows on to wooden skewers, alternating the colours.
Don't forget to leave at least 1 ½ inches at each end, so you will be able to pick the kebab up.

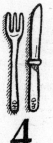

4

4 Put the kebabs on the grill rack. (TIP: Line the grill pan with tin foil – this makes washing-up a lot easier.)

5 Brush the fruit and marshmallows with melted butter. Sprinkle the rest of the brown sugar over the top.

6 Turn the grill on. When it is hot, put the grill pan under the grill. (Don't forget to use oven gloves.) Grill for one minute and remove from the heat.

7 Place a kebab on each plate and serve with the creme fraiche sauce.

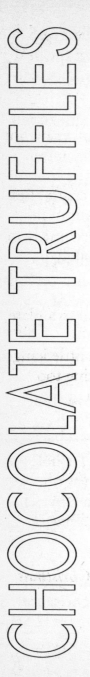

CHOCOLATE TRUFFLES

INGREDIENTS

1 oz/25 gms unsalted butter,
cut into small pieces
3 tbls double cream
7 oz/200 gms plain chocolate
2 tbls cocoa powder
icing sugar

1 Break the chocolate into small
pieces and put in a medium
sized, heat-proof bowl. Put
¾ pint of water in a
saucepan. Bring the water to
the boil over a medium heat.
Remove from the stove and
place on a heat-proof surface.

2 Put the bowl with the chocolate over the saucepan, so that the heat from the water melts the chocolate. It will take a little time.

3 Take the bowl off the saucepan. Stir the chocolate and add the butter. Stir well until all the butter has melted. Then stir in the cream. Put the bowl into the fridge until the chocolate mixture has become firm (this will take approximately 1 hour).

4 Put the cocoa powder on to a plate.

5 Dust your hands with a little icing sugar (to stop them getting too sticky). Take a teaspoon of the chocolate mixture and roll it between your hands into a ball-shape. Roll the ball in the cocoa powder until it is completely coated. Continue until all the mixture has been made into truffles.

These make wonderful Christmas or birthday presents.

INGREDIENTS

6 oz/175 gms
butter/margarine
6 oz/175 gms castor sugar
3 eggs
6 oz/175 gms self raising flour
½ tsp vanilla or almond
essence
green and red food colouring
8 oz/225 gms icing sugar
2 tbls warm water

1 Preheat the oven. Lightly
grease a 7 inch cake tin.

2 Draw a circle round the cake
tin on to a sheet of grease-
proof paper. Cut out the
circle, lightly grease the paper
and place it in the cake tin.

52

160°C
325°F
Gas M3

3 Put the butter (softened in the oven for a minute) and the sugar into a bowl. Beat the two together really well with a wooden spoon until they become pale and fluffy. Add the vanilla essence.

4 Add one egg at a time and a dessertspoonful of the measured, sifted flour. Beat each in as hard as you can. Add the rest of the sifted flour and stir it in very gently.

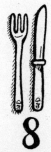

5 Divide the mixture into three. Leave one third in your mixing bowl. Put the other two sections into separate bowls. Add a few drops of green colouring to one and stir in gently. Add some red colouring to the other.

6 So you have some red, some green and some yellow mixture. Cover the base of your prepared cake tin with spoonfuls of the various colours. Don't worry if it all looks a little messy. It will come together when it is cooking.

7 Bake for 1 hour.
(To test if it is done, prick the cake

with a cocktail stick. If it comes out clean, it is done. If it comes away slightly covered with cake mixture then put the cake back for a couple of minutes. It is better to undercook slightly than have an overcooked, rock hard cake!)

8 Take the cake out of the oven. Leave it in the tin for 5 minutes, then turn it out on to a cooling rack.

9 Sift the icing sugar into a bowl and add 2 tbls warm water. Mix these into a paste. When the cake is cool, spoon the paste over it and spread it flat with a palette knife.

Your guests will have a surprise when they cut into the cake!

INGREDIENTS

7oz/198 gms tuna fish (1 tin)
4oz/100 gms soft curd cheese
2 tsp lemon juice
1 stick celery (optional)
¼ tsp salt and pepper

1 Open the can of tuna and drain off the liquid.

2 Put tuna fish, cheese, lemon juice and salt and pepper into a mixing bowl and mash with a fork.

3 Chop the celery as finely as you can and add it to the mixture.

4 Leave in the fridge for one hour before serving.

MACARONI CHEESE

INGREDIENTS

6 oz/175 gms macaroni
½ tsp salt
1 pint milk
2 oz/50 gms butter/margarine
2 oz/50 gms plain flour
¼ tsp salt and pepper
6 oz/175 gms grated cheese
1 tsp English mustard
1 medium onion, chopped
(optional)

1 Cook the pasta in boiling, salted water for 15 minutes. (If you are using the quick-cook variety, check the cooking times on the packet.)

2 While the pasta is cooking, make the sauce. Melt the butter in a saucepan and gently fry the onion until transparent. Stir in the flour and cook for 1 minute.

3 Gradually add the milk, stirring all the time. If you find it is going lumpy, take the pan off the heat and beat the mixture very firmly. Then return the pan to the stove and add more milk.

4 When all the milk has been added and you have achieved a very smooth sauce, add the mustard and salt and pepper to taste. Next add half the grated cheese.

5 Drain the macaroni and add it to the sauce. Stir them all together and pour into an ovenproof dish. Sprinkle the rest of the cheese over the top. Bake for 20 minutes in the preheated oven.

You can brown the top under a hot grill.

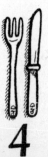

SPAGHETTI BOLOGNESE

INGREDIENTS

Allow 3 oz/75 gms of spaghetti per person (to cook see page 28)
Sauce:

1 lb/450 gms lean mince beef
3 oz/75 gms bacon, finely chopped
1 onion, finely chopped
9 oz/250 gms tin tomatoes
1 tbls tomato puree
1 tbls oil
1 clove garlic/1 heaped tsp garlic puree
1 tsp oregano
salt and pepper
1 beef stock cube dissolved in 2 tbls warm water
Parmesan cheese

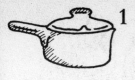

1 Heat the oil in a frying pan. Add the onions and garlic and cook until soft. Add the bacon and fry for one minute. Add the mince and brown (see page 21).

2 Transfer this into a saucepan. Add the tomatoes, tomato puree, oregano and dissolved beef stock. Season and stir well together.

3 Leave on a low heat for 30 minutes, stirring occasionally.

4 Serve on top of the spaghetti, sprinkled with Parmesan cheese.

You can leave spaghetti to stand in the water for about 10 minutes after it has cooked, if you are not ready to serve. After that it will start to go soggy.

INGREDIENTS

(per person)
2 eggs
1 tsp water
pinch salt and pepper
1 tsp butter
1 oz/25 gms chopped ham
(optional)
½ oz/10 gms grated cheese

1 Break the eggs into a bowl
   and mix with a fork. Add the
   salt and pepper, ham and
   water.

2 Melt the butter in a frying pan
   over a gentle heat. When the

60

butter is hot and frothy, pour in the mixture.

3 Cook for half a minute, then push the edges into the middle to form folds. Keep repeating this until all the egg has set.

4 Sprinkle on the grated cheese. Fold the omelette in half and slide on to a warm plate.

2

To cook a perfect omelette does take practice, but once you can do it, it makes the quickest, most delicious meal. You can put practically anything into one. Invent your own speciality!

1

CARROT & ORANGE SOUP

INGREDIENTS

¾ oz/15 gms butter
1 medium onion
¾ lb/350 gms carrots or 2
large tins
1 chicken stock cube
dissolved in ¾ pint of water
¼ pint single cream
juice of 2 oranges
chopped parsley (optional)
salt and pepper

1 Fry the onions in the butter
until transparent.

2 Peel the carrots, slice off the
ends, and chop them into
small pieces.

62

3 Put the carrot, dissolved chicken stock and onions into a saucepan. Bring slowly to the boil.

4 Boil for 15-20 minutes, with the lid on, until the carrots are well cooked.

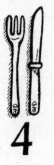

5 Place a sieve over a mixing bowl. Pour the onion and carrot mixture through the sieve. Some of the vegetables will be left in the sieve - push as much as you can through with a wooden spoon.
If you have a food processor or liquidizer, you can process the food. Don't fill the processor too full. Do half at a time if necessary.

6 Return the soup to the saucepan and bring to the boil. Take it off the heat and add the orange juice and single cream.

Astonishingly, this tastes better with tinned carrots than with fresh. The flavour of the oranges comes through more clearly. Serve decorated with chopped parsley.

APRICOT & APPLE CRUMBLE

INGREDIENTS

1 tin apricot halves/6 fresh apricots
1 large cooking apple
2 tbls castor sugar
2 oz/50 gms plain flour
2 oz/50 gms brown sugar
2 oz/50 gms ground almonds
1 oz/25 gms butter/margarine

1 Open the can of apricots and drain, or peel and stone the fresh apricots. Chop them into small cubes. Peel and core the cooking apple and chop into similar size cubes.

2 Put the apricots and apple into a pie dish and sprinkle with 2 tbls of sugar.

3 Sift the flour and sugar into a bowl. Add the ground almonds and stir. Rub in the butter carefully so there are no large lumps of butter.

4 Pour the crumble on to the top of the fruit and spread evenly. Sprinkle brown sugar over the top. Place in the oven for 30-40 minutes.

Serve hot with ice cream or whipped cream.

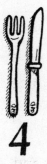

TREACLE TART

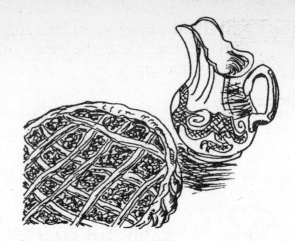

INGREDIENTS

1 block ready made shortcrust
pastry
6 tbls golden syrup
8 tbls white breadcrumbs
grated peel of ½ lemon

1 Roll out the pastry. (See
page 23.)

2 Line a 7 inch/18 cm flan dish
with the pastry, trimming the
sides and retaining the
trimmings. Bake blind. (See
page 21.)

3 Measure the golden syrup into a bowl. Grate the lemon and add to the syrup.

4 Add the breadcrumbs and mix well.

5 Pour the syrup mixture into the pastry case.

6 Roll out the pastry trimmings. Cut them into ½ inch wide strips and lay them on the top in a lattice pattern. Do not stretch the pieces over, as the pastry will shrink as it cooks.

7 Bake for 25-30 minutes.

I think this tastes best served with hot custard. You could also try cream or ice cream if you prefer.

PANCAKES

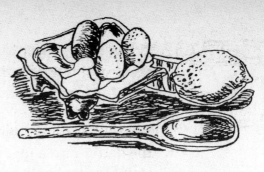

INGREDIENTS

4 oz/100 gms plain flour
¼ tsp salt
1 egg
1 egg yolk
½ pint milk
1 tbls melted butter
2 tbls cooking oil

To serve: lemon juice and castor sugar or ice cream and strawberry jam.

1 Sift the flour and salt into a bowl. Make a well in the centre of the flour and add the egg, egg yolk and half the milk. Stir the egg and milk, gradually bringing in the flour from the edges. This will take some time, but be patient. If you rush it, your batter will have lumps.

2 When all the flour is mixed in, add the rest of the milk. Mix thoroughly to form a smooth batter.

3 Stir in the melted butter and pour the batter into a jug. Leave it to stand for half an hour.

4 Dip a piece of kitchen roll into the oil. Wipe it round an omelette pan. Place the pan (non-stick if you have one) over a medium heat. Let the pan get hot (the oil will sizzle). Pour about 2 tbls of batter into the pan and tip it from side to side so the mixture coats the bottom of the pan. Cook for 1 minute.

5 When you can see the edges are cooked, use a palette knife to loosen the pancake and turn it over. If it sticks your pan was not hot enough at the beginning or the pancake was not cooked. Experiment with the first pancake and you will find the rest are easy.

6 Put the pancakes on a warm plate. Sprinkle with castor sugar and cover with foil. Serve with wedges of lemon or ice cream and jam.

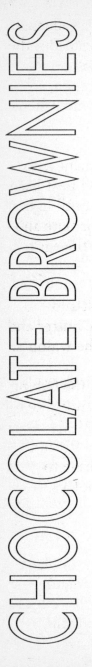

CHOCOLATE BROWNIES

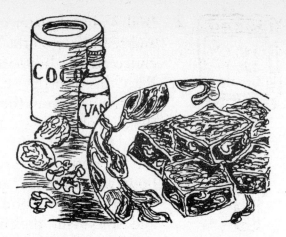

INGREDIENTS

3 oz/75 gms self raising flour
1 oz/25 gms cocoa
¼ level tsp salt
4 oz/100 gms plain chocolate broken into pieces
4 oz/100 gms soft butter/margarine
4 oz/100 gms castor sugar
2 eggs
½ tsp baking powder
½ tsp vanilla essence
2 oz/50 gms chopped walnuts (optional)

1 Grease a 10 x 8 inch/25 x 20 cm baking tray (a Swiss roll tray is ideal).

2 Boil ¾ pint of water in a saucepan and remove from the heat. Put the chocolate in a heat-proof bowl. Place this over the saucepan, so that the heat from the water melts the chocolate.

3 Put the butter or margarine into a bowl with the sugar and beat hard with a wooden spoon, until light and fluffy. Add the chocolate and vanilla essence. Beat in the eggs one at a time.

4 Sift the flour, cocoa, salt and baking powder into the butter and sugar mixture. Stir in the walnuts.

5 Turn the mixture on to the baking tray. Place in the oven and bake for 30 minutes.

6 Cut into squares, but leave to stand in the tin until cool.

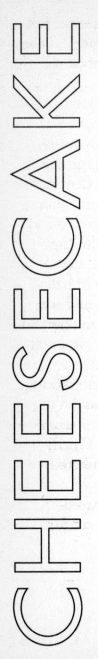

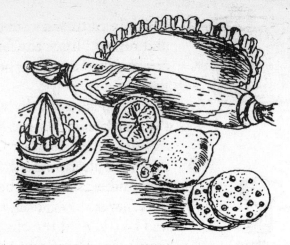

INGREDIENTS

½ lb/225 gms curd cheese
juice and grated rind of
2 lemons
14 oz/397 gm tin of
sweetened condensed full
cream milk
6 digestive biscuits
2½ oz/65 gms butter

1 Place the six digestive biscuits
into a plastic bag. Then with a
rolling pin roll over the bag,
crushing the biscuits into fine
crumbs.

2 Melt the butter in a saucepan. Put the melted butter and biscuit crumbs into a mixing bowl and stir well.

3 Press this mixture into your flan dish using the back of a wooden spoon or clean fingers. Line the base and sides. Place the dish in the fridge.

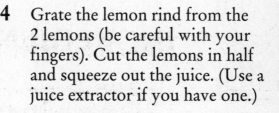

4 Grate the lemon rind from the 2 lemons (be careful with your fingers). Cut the lemons in half and squeeze out the juice. (Use a juice extractor if you have one.)

5 Beat the curd cheese with a wooden spoon to make it soft. Slowly add the sweetened condensed milk and beat it each time to make it smooth. Finally stir in the lemon juice and rind.

6 Pour this into your prepared biscuit base and leave to set for 3 hours.

LASAGNE

INGREDIENTS

1 onion, chopped
2 cloves garlic/heaped tsp
garlic puree (optional)
3 oz/75 gms cheese
1 oz/25 gms butter/oil
¾ lb/325 gms lean mince
beef
1 large tin tomatoes
½ tsp sugar
¼ tsp black pepper
½ tsp mixed herbs
¼ pint hot water
stock cube
lasagne
white sauce (see page 32)

1 Heat the oil or butter gently in a large frying pan. Fry the onion and garlic for about 5 minutes over a low heat, stirring occasionally.

2 Add the mince. Increase the heat and brown the mince all over. Remove the pan from the heat.

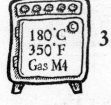

3 Dissolve the stock cube in the hot water. Add this to the mince with the tomatoes, herbs and sugar. Stir until this is all thoroughly mixed together.

4 Put to one side while you make the white sauce.

5 You are now ready to put the lasagne together. Take an oven-proof dish (approximately 20 x 25 cm/8 x 10 inches). Put half the mince in the dish and pour over half the white sauce. Cover the white sauce with sheets of lasagne. Add another layer of mince, sauce and lasagne, and then cover the top with the grated cheese.

6 Cook in the oven for 45-50 minutes.

INGREDIENTS

1 lb/450 gms extra lean mince beef
1 large tin chopped tomatoes
salt and pepper
1 tbls vinegar
1 medium onion
1 clove garlic, crushed (optional)
1 small green pepper (optional)
1 large tin red kidney beans
½ oz/10 gms butter/1 tbls cooking oil
1 tbls tomato puree
1 beef stock cube dissolved in 3 tbls hot water
½ tsp chilli powder (add a little at a time and taste)

76

220°C
425 F
Gas M7

1 Melt the butter in a frying pan and add the chopped onions. Fry the onions, stirring gently for about 5 minutes.

2 Slice the green pepper, removing all the seeds and white pith from the middle. Add the pepper and garlic to the onions and fry for a further 2 minutes.

3

3 Increase the heat and add the mince. Brown the meat, turning all the time so it doesn't burn.

4 Transfer this to a casserole dish and add the tomatoes, tomato puree, vinegar, salt and pepper, dissolved stock and chilli powder.

4

5 Stir well. Bring the mixture slowly to the boil. Place in the preheated oven and cook for 30 minutes. Then add the strained kidney beans and cook for a further 10 minutes.

WARNING Red kidney beans are poisonous unless cooked properly. (see page 83)

INGREDIENTS

4 chicken breast, skinned
2 oz/50 gms butter
1 clove garlic, crushed
1 tsp thyme
juice of ½ lemon
¼ pint double cream
1½ tbls plain flour
6 oz/175 gms mushrooms,
sliced

1 Put a very large sheet of tin
   foil in a roasting tin.

2 Melt 1 oz/25 gms of butter in
   a frying pan. Add the crushed
   garlic and the thyme. When
   you can hear the butter

78

bubbling, add the chicken breasts and brown on each side. Place the chicken on the tin foil and season with salt and pepper.

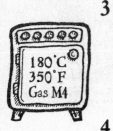

3 Add the mushrooms to the same frying pan, add the other ounce of butter and fry. Pour in the lemon juice and let it bubble. Sprinkle on the flour and cook for one minute.

4 Spoon the mixture over the chicken. Pour over the double cream.

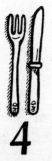

5 Wrap the edges of the tin foil together. Bake in the oven for 1 hour.

6 When it is cooked, unwrap the tin foil very carefully. Pour the contents into a warm serving dish.

CHEESE FONDUE

INGREDIENTS

Serves 8

½ pint milk
1 lb/450 gm cream cheese
2 oz/50 gm Parmesan cheese
¼ tsp salt
garlic (optional)

1 Put the cream cheese into a bowl and soften with a wooden spoon. Gradually add the milk until blended.

2 Heat the cheese and milk slowly on a medium heat. Add the salt and Parmesan cheese. Do not let it boil.

3   Pour the cheese into a fondue pot,
    over a fondue holder.

4   All the food for a fondue should
    be bite-sized.

    Here are some ideas:
        French bread
        Hardboiled eggs
        Cherry tomatoes
        Mushrooms
        Celery
        Carrots
        Apples
        Pears
        Grapes
        Prawns
        Cooked chicken

5   Using fondue forks to pick up the
    bread or vegetables, pop them into
    the fondue and coat with cheese
    sauce.

*There is a tradition that if you
drop something into the fondue,
you have to kiss the person on your
right!*

VEGETARIAN RISOTTO

INGREDIENTS

1 medium onion, chopped
1 clove garlic (optional)
1 red pepper, de-seeded and chopped
3 oz/75 gms mushrooms, sliced
2 tbls oil
1 mug easy cook rice
2 tbls frozen peas
7oz/200 gms can of red kidney beans
2 oz/50 gms peanuts
1 tsp mixed herbs
salt and pepper
1 vegetable stock cube dissolved in 2 mugs of hot water
grated cheese (optional)

1 Heat the oil in a saucepan or frying pan with a lid, and add the chopped onion, garlic and herbs. Cook slowly for 2 minutes, turning often. Add the mushrooms and stir in the rice.

2 Dissolve the stock cube in hot water and add to the pan with the other ingredients. Bring to the boil.

3 Put the lid on the pan, turn the heat down to the lowest level and cook for 25 minutes. Remove the lid and stir until all the liquid has disappeared.

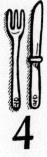

Serve with grated cheese.

4

WARNING Red kidney beans are poisonous unless soaked and cooked properly. That is why I have suggested tinned beans, which have been pre-soaked.

INGREDIENTS

4 egg yolks
4 egg whites
6 oz/175 gms castor sugar
finely grated rind and juice
of 1 lemon
finely grated rind and juice
of 1 orange
½ pint double cream

1 Separate the egg yolks and whites (see page 19).

2 Put the egg yolks and sugar into a bowl and whisk with a balloon whisk until thick and creamy. This is quite hard

84

work, but it is important that they are whisked well at this point.

3 Gradually whisk in the finely grated orange and lemon rind. Then add the orange and lemon juice one tablespoon at a time and whisk after each addition.

4 In a separate bowl whisk the double cream until it just holds its shape - that means when you scoop up a spoonful it doesn't fall off the spoon immediately. Fold this into the orange mixture.

5 Put the egg whites into a clean, dry bowl. Take a clean, dry balloon whisk (it must be very clean and dry or the egg whites will not whisk). Whisk the egg whites until they just hold their shape and fold these into the cream and orange-and-lemon mixture, using a metal spoon.

6 Pour the mixture into a pint mixing bowl, cover tightly and freeze overnight.

INGREDIENTS

4 oz/100 gms plain chocolate
3 egg yolks
3 egg whites
double cream to serve

1 Pour ¾ pint water into a saucepan and bring to the boil. Remove from the heat and put on a heat-proof surface.

2 Break the chocolate into small pieces in a heat-proof mixing bowl and put the mixing bowl over the saucepan of hot water. Stir occasionally. When the chocolate has melted

86

remove the bowl from the pan, add the egg yolks and stir well.

3   Put the egg whites into a clean bowl and with a clean whisk, whisk the egg whites until they are very stiff.

4   Add one heaped tablespoon of egg white to the mixture and stir in with a wooden spoon. Add the rest and fold it in carefully with a rubber spatula. It is the egg white that gives the chocolate the mousse-like consistency. If you stir too hard, you will knock out all the air bubbles.

5   Pour the mixture into a soufflé dish or a pretty bowl and leave it in the fridge overnight to set.

You could cover the top of the mouse with grated plain or milk chocolate. Or you could decorate the mousse with fruit or cream.

FRENCH APPLE FLAN

INGREDIENTS

9oz/250 gms ready made puff
pastry
1 ½ lb/700 gms golden
delicious apples (approx 6)
peeled and cored
2 heaped tbls castor sugar
2 tbls water
½ tsp cinnamon
½ jar apricot jam

1 Grease a medium-sized
baking tray.

2 Put a block of puff pastry on
a floured work surface. Roll
out the pastry (see page 20)
until you have an oblong
slightly smaller than your
baking tray. Trim the edges
straight. Place it on the baking
sheet and leave to rest.

3 Chop 4 apples into quarters.

Place these in a small saucepan with two tbls of water. Place over a low heat for 20 minutes, stirring occasionally. Take the pan off the heat. Add the cinnamon and one heaped tbls of sugar. Mash and leave to cool slightly.

4 Cut the remaining two apples into quarters. Slice each quarter lengthways into thin slices.

5 Spoon the apple mixture into the middle of the pastry. Spread it out , leaving an inch all the way round.

3

6 Arrange the apple slices in overlapping lines, covering all the apple mixture. Sprinkle the apples with the remaining sugar. Place in a the preheated oven for 25 minutes or until the pastry is well risen.

7 Put the apricot jam into a saucepan with a tablespoon of water and put it on a low heat. Stir this until all the jam has turned to liquid. Paint the liquid jam over your tart to give a lovely golden gloss to the apples and pastry.

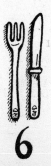

6

BANOFFI PIE

INGREDIENTS

8 oz/225gms ready-made
shortcrust pastry
14 oz/400 gms can full cream
sweetened condensed milk
2 large bananas
½ pint double cream

1 Boil the can of condensed
milk for 2 hours. Make sure
the pan does not boil dry and
stays covered with water.
Allow the tin to become
completely cold before you
open it.

(It is sensible to boil two or three tins at the same time as they will last in your storecupboard for a long time. The next time you want to make Banoffi Pie you will have a tin ready.)

180°C
350°F
Gas M4

2 Roll out the shortcrust pastry. Use it to line an 8 inch/20cm flan dish and bake blind (see page 21).

3 Open the cold can of condensed milk and spoon the contents into the flan case.

4 Peel the bananas, slice and use them to cover the toffee mixture.

3

5 Whip the double cream until it is light and fluffy. Spread it over the bananas and toffee mixture and serve.

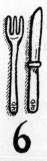

6

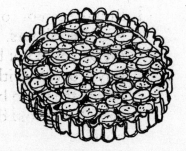

PAVLOVA

INGREDIENTS

3 egg whites (you get better
volume if you separate the
eggs the day before)
6 oz/175 gms castor sugar
2 tsp cornflour
1 tsp white vinegar
¼ tsp vanilla essence
½ pint double cream

Any combination of fruit eg.
raspberries, strawberries, grapes etc.

1 Draw a circle on grease-proof
   paper, using a large plate as a
   guide. Put this paper on a
   baking tray.

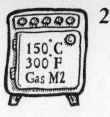

2   Put the egg whites into a clean, dry bowl and whisk until they are stiff. Add the sugar spoonful by spoonful, whisking each time, until half the sugar has been mixed in.

3   Fold in the remaining sugar with a metal spoon and add the cornflour, vinegar and vanilla essence.

4   Pile the meringue mixture on to the grease-proof paper, using the circle as a guide. Push in the middle with a mixing bowl. This gives a good shape to fill with the cream and fruit.

5   Cook for 1½ hours. Carefully peel the meringue off the paper and place it on a serving dish. Whip the double cream and pile it into the meringue. Put the fruit on top and serve.

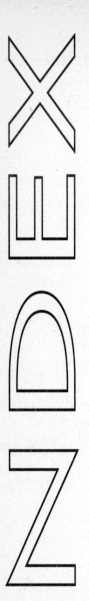

First published in Great Britain
in 1992 by Hodder &
Stoughton

British Library C.I.P.

A catalogue record for this
title is available from the
British Library

ISBN 0 340 57661 8

Printed and bound in Great Britain
for Hodder and Stoughton
Children's Books, a division of
Hodder and Stoughton Ltd., Mill
Road, Dunton Green, Sevenoaks,
Kent TN13 2YA (Editorial Office:
47 Bedford Square, London WC1B
3DP) by Clays Ltd, St Ives plc.